Contents

Places and spaces

The Sydney Opera House is … one of the great … buildings of the 20th century, … known throughout the world – a symbol for not only a city, but a whole country and a continent. The Pritzker Prize, 2003

Australia has many unique places and spaces. People have influenced these places and spaces in many different ways.

When developing buildings, such as houses, schools and shops, to meet our basic needs, or developing means of travel, such as roads and railways, many things need to be considered. These include issues of safety, and disability access.

Art spaces, sports venues and **landmark** buildings are also created. These can shape the cultural identity of a place and some become famous, such as the Sydney Opera House.

Climate and landscape also have an effect on places. Buildings are designed to keep the heat in or out, depending on their location, or are constructed from different materials.

Sometimes, one need, such as more housing, might override another, such as preserving a green space. When people disagree on these decisions, protests can occur.

Did you know?
Federation Square is a popular public space with an unusual design. Some people argue the **contemporary** architecture doesn't fit with the historic buildings nearby. It was even awarded 'Fifth ugliest building in the world'!

LET'S FIND OUT

- Which human needs shape where we live?
- What gives places a unique cultural identity?
- How can we minimise our impact on the natural landscape around us?
- How does climate influence the way we build our towns and cities?
- How do we manage and preserve our special places?

landmark a well-known human or natural feature
contemporary modern

A section of Federation Square, Melbourne, Victoria

At home with the environment

Australia is a country of diverse climates and unique landforms. Reporter Callum Bruce roams Australia to discover some of the ways people have influenced their local places and spaces to build homes.

Underground life

First stop, Coober Pedy, a town in northern South Australia, about halfway between Adelaide and Alice Springs. It's famous for the mining of precious gems called opals. In summer, the temperature in Coober Pedy soars. It reached a temperature of 45.1°C in 2012!

When you wander around the town, it is very different from other places. Front doors are evident in the rock faces everywhere. These lead into special underground homes called dugouts.

People inhabit these underground homes to keep cool. Local resident Mick Bailey claims, "Dugouts are cheaper to construct than regular homes, as fewer building materials are needed. Living in a dugout is the simplest and cheapest way of keeping the sun out!" There's no need for air conditioning in a dugout either, because they usually stay a constant temperature of around 24°C.

A Coober Pedy dugout

Crocodile Harry

Many tourists who come to Coober Pedy visit the 'Crocodile's Nest', the home of Crocodile Harry, who died in 2006. His dugout home is decorated with photos of him catching crocodiles, and many unique artworks. His home was used in the film *Mad Max Beyond Thunderdome*.

Up on stilts

In Queensland, instead of living underground to suit the climate, many people live in homes built on stilts. This unique style of living has many benefits for the locals.

1 Extreme weather

Stilt homes are a great way of adapting to the weather, which is hot and humid for much of the year, with heavy rainfall at times. Being raised off the ground assists with keeping houses cool. It can also help prevent houses from being flooded during heavy rain.

2 Unwanted visitors

Having a house on stilts also helps prevent termites from attacking the house and destroying the roof timber. There are many dangerous snakes in Queensland, which like to shelter in cool, dry homes. Having a house above the ground helps keep these unwanted visitors out.

3 Handy space

The area underneath these homes is a useful place for a laundry or storing equipment, such as lawnmowers. The space can be a handy alternative to building a shed. In rural areas, the space can be used to stockpile wood, but beware – woodpiles underneath houses are a favourite spot for snakes to shelter in!

A typical Queensland home

Stilt walking!

In the Daintree Rainforest in Queensland, a walkway has been constructed on massive stilts. It has been designed to have little impact on the environment and takes visitors through each level of the forest **canopy**.

canopy the leafy cover over the forest plants beneath it

The sky's the limit

Far from the rainforest and desert, Sydney, New South Wales, has a stunning skyline with high-rise apartments, **iconic** buildings and spectacular skyscrapers, where many corporations and businesses have their offices.

High-rise apartments allow many people to live within the hectic city space. They have thick glass to keep the city noise out, and air conditioning, so there is no need to open the windows. There are lifts to travel many floors and fire escapes for safety. Some have a swimming pool, or an amazing rooftop garden with a vegetable patch and a sundeck.

Eco-skyscraper

Sydney is also home to 1 Bligh Street, an award-winning office structure. It is famous for being Australia's first eco-skyscraper.

It has many sustainable features, such as rooftop solar panels that convert sunlight to energy. The **sewerage plant** in the basement recycles 90 per cent of the building's wastewater, and the air conditioning is powered by a massive chilled beam. On the outside, there is an extra layer of sunshades that can move to different angles to reflect the sun, and keep the heat and glare away.

Up, up and away!
Q1, on the Gold Coast in Queensland, is the tallest residential building in the Southern Hemisphere. At 322.5 metres tall, it is also the fifth tallest building in the world!

1 Bligh Street, Australia's first eco-skyscraper

---

iconic a memorable image that has come to symbolise something
sewerage plant a place where wastewater is treated

Breakaway tasks

Remembering

1 What are the underground homes in Coober Pedy called?

2 List three reasons why people in Queensland build their houses on stilts.

Understanding

3 Complete this chart in your notebook, listing the positive and negative points about living in a dugout home, a stilt home and a high-rise apartment.

	Positives	Negatives
Dugout home		
Stilt home		
High-rise apartment		

4 Write a paragraph on why 1 Bligh Street, Sydney, is known as an eco-skyscraper.

Applying

5 Draw a picture or diagram of a landmark building in your state or territory. Label the features that make it so special.

Analysing

6 Locate 1 Bligh Street on a map of Sydney. Identify three other landmarks on the map and explain what makes them landmarks.

7 Draw or trace a map of Australia and mark the location of Coober Pedy, Sydney, the Gold Coast and the Daintree Rainforest. Research two other places where people have influenced the natural features of the area. Locate them on your map and mark them. Include a short description.

Evaluating

8 Brainstorm with a partner ways that the landscape or climate has influenced the style of buildings in your area. Present your ideas as an oral report with images.

9 Research some features that could be included to make your school building more eco-friendly. Create a diagram of your school with these eco-friendly features.

Creating

10 Plan and write a narrative about living in one of the places featured in the report.

Park life

This is one person's response to a local **council** survey, sent to households in the area.

Petts Hill Council is conducting a short survey in relation to pet dogs at Redgum Park. The survey results will help the council to continue supporting visitors to the park, and ensure the park is an enjoyable space for everyone.

Please respond to the questions below.

1 Are you male or female?
- Male [x]
- Female [ ]

2 What is your age?
- 0–18 [x]
- 19–40 [ ]
- 41–60 [ ]
- 61+ [ ]

3 How often do you visit the park?
- Daily [x]
- Weekly [ ]
- Monthly [ ]
- Occasionally [ ]

4 Which activities do you do at the park?
- Jog [ ]
- Walk [x]
- Cycle [x]
- Picnic [x]
- Sit on the benches [ ]
- Play sport [x]
- Use the playground [ ]
- Other [ ]

5 Do you ever walk a dog at the park? (If No, go to question 9)
- Yes [x]
- No [ ]

6 Do you walk your dog on or off the leash at the park?
- On the leash [ ]
- Off the leash [ ]
- Both [x]

7 Where in the park do you walk your dog?
- On the grass areas [x]
- On the paths [x]
- In the playground [ ]
- On the oval [ ]
- Near the BBQs [ ]

8 Do you clean up your dog's waste at the park?
- Always [ ]
- Occasionally [x]
- Never [ ]

council government body in charge of local affairs

9 How often do you notice dog waste on the ground at the park?

Always ☑

Occasionally ☐

Never ☐

10 Have you ever found a dog to be a nuisance at the park?

Yes ☑

No ☐

Comments:

A dog tried to steal food from our picnic once. The owner had to drag him away, but dogs do ADORE sausages! Another time, my friend skidded in dog poo while attempting to save a goal during soccer practice – gross!

11 Do you think the park rules are obvious to dog owners?

Yes ☐

No ☑

Comments:

I wasn't aware of any rules! I haven't noticed any signs or notices around the park.

12 Would you support an off-leash area for dogs in the park?

Yes ☑

No ☐

Comments:

This would be great, as it would stop dogs getting in the way of runners, and people could picnic in peace. It would also be an awesome place for dogs to play freely.

13 Would you support dog-related events at the park?

Yes ☑

No ☐

Comments:

It would be fun to take part in a big charity dog walk.

14 What suggestions do you have for ways Petts Hill Council could improve dog facilities at the park?

More dog poo bins and free plastic bags. Some dog training sessions in the off-leash area would be fun for owners, and could assist with better dog behaviour.

Breakaway tasks

Remembering

1 Why doesn't the person responding to the survey think the park rules are clear?

2 Describe the experience the person had of a dog being a nuisance at the park.

Understanding

3 Discuss in small groups why someone jogging might find the dogs in the park to be a problem.

4 Discuss with a partner whether providing free plastic bags is a way of improving the dog facilities in the park and list some other ideas.

Applying

5 Complete the survey yourself in relation to your local park. Compare your response to a partner's.

Analysing

6 Describe what you think the actual purpose is of the survey. Give evidence to support your view.

7 Write a profile of the person who completed this survey and their dog. Include a picture of the person and their dog.

8 Discuss with a partner what rules might be needed at a busy park. Think about all the different areas (such as the playground, car park and oval), and design a list of eight park rules to go on the council website.

Evaluating

9 Conduct a survey in your class about what people do at the local park. Draw a pie chart to show the results.

Creating

10 Design your ideal park. Make a list of ten features you might find there. Draw a map of the park, considering the best place for each of these features. Label each feature.

Beach wheels

13th November

Sofia Davis
19 Duggan Street
South Perth WA 6000

Buzzy Beach Council
31 Wave Road
Seacrest WA 6015

Dear Madam/Sir,

As you are currently planning how to improve the saltwater beach pool, I am writing with some ideas.

I use a wheelchair to get around. At the moment, it's extremely difficult for me and other people with special needs to access the pool. Here's why:

1. When it's busy, it's impossible to park near the access path to the pool. We often have to park on the far side of the car park and it's tricky **manoeuvring** my wheelchair through the gravel to reach the access path.
2. The access path to the pool is rocky. Occasionally, my wheelchair becomes wedged in a crack, and I get stuck. It can be a challenging, bumpy ride.
3. The steps into the pool are very steep and slippery, making it dangerous when I pull myself up and down.

My solutions:

1. The car spaces closest to the entry path should be marked for disabled access to keep them free for disabled users.
2. A wooden walkway should be constructed over the rocky entry path to make it easier for people with special needs to move across.
3. A ramp into the pool should be constructed for safer and easier access.

Please consider these solutions. They will make the pool a more **inclusive** and safer place.

Yours sincerely,

Sofia Davis (aged 11)

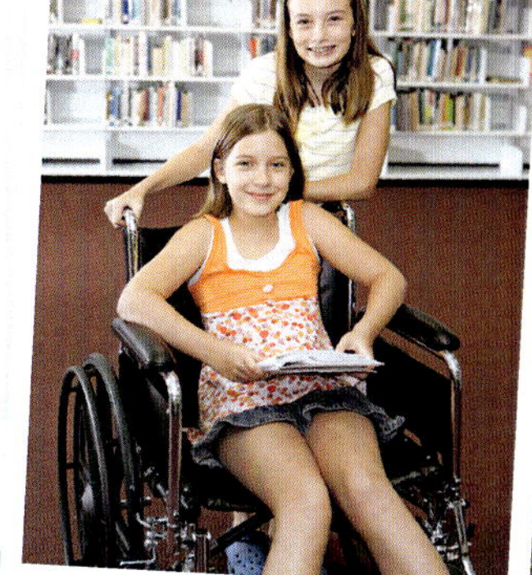

manoeuvring moving
inclusive giving everyone entry, regardless of disability for example

Breakaway tasks

Remembering

1 List two reasons why the pool is difficult for people with special needs to access.

2 How does Sofia suggest the pool area could be improved?

Understanding

3 Draw and label a diagram of the area with the changes Sofia proposed in her letter.

Applying

4 How might Buzzy Beach pool be a challenge for a vision-impaired person? Write a letter to the council from the point of view of a vision-impaired person, suggesting improvements to the area.

Analysing

5 Identify the main arguments for or against Sofia's ideas. Discuss them with a partner.

6 Create a survey about the Buzzy Beach pool to find out how the area could be improved. You can use Sofia's ideas as a starting point.

7 Discuss other ways the council could improve the car park to make access easier.

Evaluating

8 Discuss with a partner whether you think Sofia's letter is convincing. Consider how the council might respond to her ideas. Write a letter in reply from the council to Sofia's letter.

9 Research the facilities at a sports venue in your local area. Write a report explaining why the facilities are ideal for use by the public or ways that they need to be improved.

Creating

10 Look at the health and safety issues in and around your school. Draw a diagram labelling the areas where students need to take special care, such as near the canteen or at the school crossing. Use your information to create a poster for display with one health and safety message you have identified.

Don't climb Uluru!

Each year, thousands of tourists visit Uluru, the incredible sandstone rock formation in the middle of Australia that is sacred to the Anangu traditional owners. Some people decide to climb it; others decide not to climb it. The Australian Government Department of the Environment website provides guidance to visitors about making this decision.

Please don't climb

> *"That's a really important sacred thing that you are climbing … You shouldn't climb. It's not the real thing about this place. The real thing is listening to everything."*
>
> Traditional owner

Anangu traditional owners of Uluru-Kata Tjuta National Park have a responsibility to teach and safeguard visitors to our land. We feel great sadness when a person dies or is hurt on our land. We would like to educate people on the reasons we ask you not to climb and if you choose to climb, we ask that you do so safely.

Cultural reasons

We ask visitors not to climb Uluru because of its spiritual significance as the traditional route of the ancestral Mala men on their arrival at Uluru. We prefer that visitors explore Uluru through the wide range of guided walks and interpretive attractions on offer in the park. At the Cultural Centre you will learn more about these, and about the significance of Uluru in Anangu culture.

Safety reasons

The climb is physically demanding and can be dangerous. At least 35 people have died while attempting to climb Uluru and many others have been injured. At 346 metres, Uluru is higher than the Eiffel Tower, as high as a 95-storey building. The climb is very steep and can be very slippery. It can be very hot at any time of the year and strong wind gusts can hit the summit or slopes at any time.

ancestral something belonging to ancestors (people we are related to from the past)

interpretive something that provides an explanation

National Parks. Uluru – Kata Tjuta publications

Every year people are rescued by park rangers, many suffering serious injuries such as broken bones, heat exhaustion and extreme **dehydration**.

Environmental reasons

There are also significant environmental impacts of climbing Uluru. If you have a close look you can see the path is smooth from millions of footsteps since the 1950s. This **erosion** is changing the face of Uluru.

Also, there are no toilet facilities on top of Uluru, and no soil to dig a hole. You can imagine what happens many times a day when the climb is open. When it rains, everything gets washed off the rock and into the waterholes where precious reptiles, birds, animals and frogs live. A water quality study at Uluru has found **significantly** higher **bacterial** levels in the waterholes fed by runoff from the climb site, compared to those further away.

Uluru is spectacular at sunrise.

dehydration suffering from a lack of water
erosion wearing away of rock
significantly importantly
bacterial relating to bacteria, which are types of living things that can cause infection

Breakaway tasks

Remembering

1 List five reasons why the Anangu traditional owners ask people not to climb Uluru.

Understanding

2 With a partner, discuss what the traditional owner means when he says climbing is 'not the real thing about this place'?

3 Record your ideas on why some people still choose to climb Uluru, and share them with your classmates.

Applying

4 Draw or trace a map of Australia and label Uluru. Research its geographical features and prepare a fact file.

5 Research the Creation stories of the Anangu traditional owners and the route of the ancestral Mala men. Prepare an information report.

Analysing

6 Conduct a survey to find out whether people think it's right or wrong to climb Uluru. Draw a graph to show the results.

7 Research and create a webpage or poster featuring other ways that visitors could explore Uluru, rather than climbing.

Evaluating

8 Research and locate some other sites that are sacred to Indigenous peoples. Write a magazine article featuring one of these places.

Creating

9 Select a place that is special to you. Write a speech persuading others to treat that place with respect. Perform your speech for the class.

10 Research some photos and draw a picture of Uluru. Make a list of adjectives that describe how you think it might look and feel to be there. Write a poem about Uluru.

Strands in action

Core tasks

1 Prepare a proposal to the council for a new bike track in your area.
- Create a survey to determine the best location.
- In your proposal, include a list of the benefits it will bring to the area.
- Draw a map of the bike track and label some of the features that cyclists will encounter on the ride.

2 Your favourite park is being redeveloped. Write the script for a television news report about a campaign to save it. Plan your script:
- Explain why the park is being redeveloped and by whom.
- Explain why it is important to save the park.
- Include interviews with the protesters and the developers.
- Take some photos or draw diagrams of the area.
- Present your news report to the class.

Extra tasks

1 Design a poster to advertise a popular spot in your local area.

2 Interview four classmates to find out whether they think any improvements could be made to the outdoor areas around your school. Write a report about your findings.

3 Research and write a list of guidelines for the public about how to minimise their impact on the environment while camping in the bush.

4 Find out about a local development. Prepare a T-chart for and against this development.

When writing survey questions, make sure they are clearly written in simple language, without jargon or technical terms. It is also important to check your questions are not 'loaded'. This is when the words you use in the question encourage people to respond in a certain way.